REEDHAM MEMORIES

Sheila Hutchinson

Sheila Hutchinson

LIMITED EDITION

Front Cover Photograph:
Steam train on the Reedham Swing Bridge circa 1950. Supplied by Julie Layton and taken by her late father John Debbage.

Back Cover Photograph:
Berney Arms High Mill, circa 1960. Supplied by Mike Pickard.

ISBN 9780954168353

Published
By
Sheila & Paul Hutchinson
7 Colman Avenue,
Stoke Holy Cross,
Norwich,
Norfolk.
NR14 8NA

Printed
By
RPD Litho Printers
Gorleston
Norfolk

INTRODUCTION

I lived at the Berney Arms hamlet, which is part of the Reedham Parish.

This book is a companion book for the earlier books 'Reedham Remembered' and 'Berney Arms Remembered'.

With the help of the Reedham folk, some of which live there now and some who have moved away, supplying me with their old photographs, and some with memories, I have been able to produce this book.

The Berney Arms photographs are at the end of the book. Some of the history of Reedham and Berney Arms can be found in 'Reedham Remembered' and 'Berney Arms Remembered'.

Figure 1. Postcard view of the river showing the first Reedham Swing Bridge. The bridge was built in 1847 and replaced in 1904. Supplied by Mike Browne.

Figure 2. View through the Reedham Swing Bridge. Supplied by Malcolm Cushion.

Figure 3. Top: Steam engine approaching the Swing Bridge.

Bottom: View of the Lowestoft Norwich line from Maypole Hill with Mutton's Coal Store and the New Cut in the centre background circa 1940's. Supplied by Myra and Sony Horton.

Figure 4. Two views of Reedham Swing Bridge circa 1950 taken by the late John Debbage. The Swing Bridge 'Tin' Cottages on the Raveningham side of the river are shown on the left of the bottom photograph. Supplied by Julie Layton, nee Debbage.

JULIE LAYTON (NEE DEBBAGE) & BROTHER PHILIP DEBBAGE: 'MEMORIES OF VISITING NANNA AT THE SWING BRIDGE COTTAGES'

Figure 5. Steam trains crossing the Swing Bridge circa 1950 bythe late John Debbage, supplied by Julie Layton.

Our grandparents were Ernest Frederick and Olive Agnes Debbage. Grandfather died at the age of 54 and had been a signalman at the Reedham Swing Bridge for many years. Nanna lived in the swing bridge cottages.

We had to walk across the swing bridge to get to the cottages. They were made of corrugated metal and painted green, and lined with tongue and groove walls. There was no running water and we had to use an outside hand pump, which poured into a wooden tub. A communal outhouse was the washing room. There was a copper, which was heated by an open fire for hot water, baths, to wash and rinse in, and a mangle. There was electric lights and cooker, and a coal fire for heating in the cottage. Round the corner of the cottages was a shed behind the coalhouse, which was the toilet, on stilts with a wooden seat, and had to be emptied and buried in the garden so I was told. I remember Nanna having a large orchard of apple trees and other fruit bushes. We would help pick apples, which were then stored in wooden tea-chests. Nanna would make some lovely apple pies! I also remember looking for mushrooms on the marshes: that was great fun.

My dad would make us a bow and arrow, the bow made from tree branches and the arrows usually reeds, and we would play on the marshes opposite. In wintertime the lows on the marshes would freeze over, and we would skate on them, they were frozen solid, about six inches deep.

Mum, Dad and Nanna knew the signal-box man, his name was Ted. Sometimes on Sundays when we went to visit Nanna, Ted would fall asleep and leave the swing-bridge off! I remember us shouting and Dad throwing stones to wake him up, eventually he would hear us and put the bridge back on. Sometimes Ted would let my brother and I go up the signal-box and pull the levers to change the signals. I remember he used to catch eels in the river, they would be in bowls, skinned and de-headed. Being little, we were not sure what they were! Ted would also let us stand in the middle of the swing bridge when the bridge was in the open position to let the boats go through.

Across the marshes was a farm. A lady used to come across and brought butter for my Nanna.

Figure 6. Ernest Frederick Debbage and wife Olive Agnes photographed at No. 3 Swing Bridge Cottages in 1949, and on the Swing Bridge. He was a signalman at the Swing Bridge. Supplied by Julie Layton.

My brother and I went exploring under the signal box once and found an open well. It looked very deep so we kept away. We thought it would be fun one day to creep through the reed-bed and spy on the River Police boat and Inspector only to find he was fast asleep! We crept away again – he didn't even know!

I remember one evening, it was just getting dark, we were playing in the orchard and saw a large creature amongst the trees. Not knowing what it was we climbed up the step ladders and stayed there till Mum and Dad came to get us. Dad said it was a coypu rat.

My Nanna used to play the organ in Reedham Church, she also had a piano at home and used to give piano lessons. She would get very annoyed if we played on her piano, she used to say, 'If you can't play properly leave it alone!'

Many a Sunday was spent at Nanna's house, we had so much fun over there. We will never forget it.

Figure 7. Outside no. 3 Swing Bridge Cottages: Mabel Debbage, nee Chase, Olive Agnes Debbage, Philip Debbage, railway signalman Albert Lewis Witham, and Julie Debbage. Supplied by Julie Layton, nee Debbage.

MABEL MOORE (DEBBAGE) nee CHASE REMEMBERS:

I used to live on New Road next door to John Ewles and the fire station was opposite, so I never missed their call outs. They left in a hurry one night and one chap, I remember left his sandwich on the trailer.

My Dad Benjamin Victor Chase worked for the railway and when he was on duty for the 2 till 10 shift and the weather was fine my mother and I would visit my Uncle Arthur and Aunt Mabel Broom who lived in Beighton, just up the road from the Cantley Cock.

We would catch the train from Reedham to Cantley and then walk to Beighton. On the way we would see several people whom my mother knew. They would always have a little yarn while attending to their garden when we went by. In those days there was always quite a lot of garden to attend to, growing vegetables, potatoes were the main crop, attending to fruit bushes and perhaps an apple or pear tree. Perhaps a pump or well. The flower border usually fell to the lady of the house to see to.

In sight of Arthur and Mabel's house there was a little cottage we would

have to pass. The old boy leaning over the gate, how he knew we were coming was always a mystery, as the road would be clear, but there he would be a leaning on the gate. Being very polite and asking how everyone was, which was the done thing in those days, Mr Debbage would ask us in to the cottage. Martha had just made a little homemade wine and thought mother would like to try a glass. I had some in a cup and very nice it was too. Mum was invited to have a second glass. This wine tasting could have got out of hand, I'm sure my mum managed to 'hold her own', but not sure if we didn't roll along to Auntie's house. As Auntie would say "I suppose you have been talking to Mr Debbage!", when

Figure 8. Benjamin Victor and Kate Elizabeth Chase at New Road. Supplied by Julie Layton.

arriving. This Mr Debbage was John Debbage's grandfather, and I have often wondered how John and his parents got on when visiting. It was the custom years ago for families to visit their parents and especially on Sundays, after Church or Chapel of course.

My aunt and uncle moved from Beighton to Heckingham and so we used to go over the Ferry to visit them.

Figure 9. Steam Train crossing Reedham Swing Bridge in 1954. Supplied by Julie Layton and taken by her father the late John Debbage.

Figure10. Mrs Debbage at the Church organ. Supplied by Julie Layton.

Figure 11. Relaying tracks on the Swing Bridge 26 October 2006. Hutchinson.

Figure 12. Reedham railway staff. Top: circa 1930.

Bottom: circa 1950, from left: Station Master Mr Wright; Mr Percy Boyce, Porter; Mr Oldfield, Signalman; Mr Harry White, Signalman; Mr Fisk, Signalman; Mr Dodman, Porter; Mr Clem Spalding, Porter. Supplied by Mabel Moore, nee Chase.

Figure 13. Railway sidings between Reedham Station and Witton Bridge. Supplied by Malcolm Cushion.

Above: Steam Train Special 'The Norfolkman' passing through Reedham Station 5th May 2001. Engine 45157, 'The Glasgow Highlander'. Hutchinson

Figure 14. Left: Railwayman Clem Spalding, Mr Howard and Ben Chase. Supplied by Julie Layton.

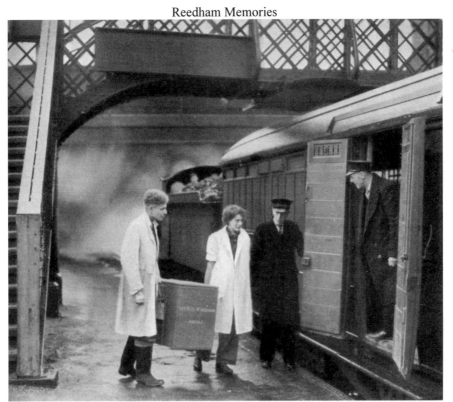

Figure 15. Pettitt's poultry goods being loaded onto the train at Reedham Station circa 1950.

ANN WOOTTON WRITES ABOUT HER HANTON ANCESTORS:

My grandfather Edward William George Hanton was born in Reedham in 1873, a son of George and Susan Hanton, nee Mallett. The Hanton family were living in one of the cottages on Low Farm Road in 1871 and George worked as a railway labourer. When Susan died, George and the family moved away from Reedham and George remarried. Edward ran away from home when he was about 10 and lived with a family at a farmhouse on the Acle Straight. Eventually after finishing school he got a job with the railway and when he married Alice Amelia Harding in 1902 he lived in Lowestoft. In about 1920, still working for the railway, Edward and family moved back to Reedham and lived in a cottage at Witton Green. Edward was forced through ill-health to take early retirement from the railways and died in 1938. My grandmother Alice died in 1948 and in her Will the cottage, which was left to Albert, her eldest son, was described as a freehold dwelling with premises valued at £550. It is interesting to note that her funeral expenses were £24.10.0d, and the Doctors fees were 8 / 6d. Alice and Edward were both buried in Reedham Churchyard.

Figure 16. Cottages at Witton Green in the mid 1920s. The cottage on the right is where Edward and Alice Hanton lived during the 1920s and 1930s. Supplied by Ann Wootton.

MICHAEL PEARSON REMEMBERS:

I was born at Reedham in 1937 at Clare Cottages next to the Railway Tavern on the Havaker. The next door neighbours were Clifford and Mary James who had two children Alan and Susan. Mary was the daughter of Mr and Mrs Carter who kept the Eagle Tavern, and Clifford was a tractor driver who worked for The East Anglia Real Property. My late father was Assistant Manager of the Co-op Stores on The Hills.

I went to Reedham School from Sept 1942 to July 1949. In 1949 I passed the 11 Plus and went daily by train to Great Yarmouth Grammar. Other boys who went to the Grammar School were Patrick Browne, whose father kept the Post Office, John Newman, who lived in a little bungalow opposite Cooling's Stores, and Barry Boast, son of the School Headmaster. When I first went to Reedham School Mrs Howard was the infant teacher, Class 2 was taken by Fred Howlett, Class 3 by Mrs Joyce Stone, and Mr Howard was the headmaster. Mr. Boast took over from Howard when he retired. When I was in Mrs Stone's class, which had double desks there was an odd number of pupils, I was the one who sat on my own so Mrs Stone let her Spaniel dog sit next to me as she used to bring her dog to school every day. At break and dinner times my job was to collect all the milk bottles up and collect all the drainings from them, which I gave to the dog to drink.

Others who lived at Witton Green were: Mr and Mrs De Caux and their daughter Jill at The Firs; he was a manager with The East Anglian Real Property at Cantley. Mr and Mrs Greenacre; he was Co-op manager and moved to Gt. Yarmouth to manage the Northgate Street shop.(Mr Arthur Scrivener then took over the Co-op at Reedham, and he lived on the Hills near the school.) Mrs Heath, who owned Clare Cottages, where I lived. Mr and Mrs Smith owned the Grocery Shop in Witton Green and they had a son Michael. Mr and Mrs Sharman and son Keith. Mr and Mrs Plummer and son Nelson: Mr Plummer used to cut hair in his shed at night time. Mr Hunt was village postman and Scout Master; I was a member of his scout group. Mr and Mrs Mace, whose son Ian was my best mate, and daughter Adele: Mr Mace worked at Cantley Sugar Factory. I remember cycling to Freethorpe and Halvergate in the summer holiday with Ian and his mother to earn money picking blackcurrants. In 1947 when we had a lot of snow Ian and I dug out a track through the snow along the Footpath from Witton Green to the Gospel Hall on the Hills.

Figure 17. Mrs Alice Hanton and Glenna Cheetham at Witton Green in 1938. Supplied by Ann Wootton.

Mr Lenny Humphrey kept the Railway Tavern and his son John kept goal for Reedham Football Club.

In the summer time all the railway carriages which used to bring the holidaymakers to Yarmouth on a Saturday were left in the railway sidings at Witton Green till the next Saturday when they took them home again. Ian Mace and I used to get into these carriages and collect cigarette boxes and match boxes as we both collected them.

In the summer holidays I used to stand on the back of the binder at Mutton's Farm when they were cutting corn with horses. Then came the tractor, a blue Fordson Major. Mr Forder drove the tractor with Mr Mutton on the binder. After the field was cut I used to help to shock up, which is standing the sheaves of corn up to dry ready for carting into the farmyard to await the steam threshing engine in the winter. Two stacks were built with room between to stand the threshing drum in the middle. The corn was carted to the farmyard by horse and cart. I was the hold gee boy riding on the horses back to move the horse and cart from one shock of corn to the next with my feet on the shafts of the cart.

The corn stacks in the farmyard were thatched by Mr Forder with reeds from the riverbank nearby to keep out the water.

Reedham Memories

In the winter I used to help the farm worker to dig sugar beet with a two pronged fork and then lay them in rows for him to chop the tops off. These were then loaded on to a horse and cart and taken to Reedham Station and loaded into trucks for despatch to Cantley Factory. The beet tops were used for feeding the cattle in the winter.

When I was about 11 years old I used to go on the bread van from the Co-op with Harold Hall round the local villages on Saturday delivering bread and grocery orders. I also worked one summer holiday at Sanderson's Boatyard doing odd jobs. I used to serve petrol to visiting cruisers; also water to the cruisers: 3 pence for small cruisers, 6d for medium sized and 1 shilling for large cruisers.

I got a job at the Co-op on Saturdays and holidays doing odd jobs. I used to go round the village delivering bread, milk, grocery orders on a trade bike. A trade bike was a bit difficult to handle, especially with a crate of 20 pints of milk over the front wheel, cornering was the most difficult. Working at the Co-op then was Mr Scrivener the manager, my late father the assistant manager, Arthur Haylett, Enid Mace who was Ian Mace's cousin, Queenie Merry who was Ian's aunt and Cecil Pearson from Halvergate (no relation of mine). Cecil eventually went to manage the Co-op at Martham and Enid Mace married Arthur Haylett.

My grandparents Mr and Mrs Gravener had lived at Reedham in a small semi-detached cottage on Riverside between the Swing Bridge and Riverside House. My grandfather was a wherryman and worked for Mr Wales who lived at Riverside House. I remember Mr Dewhurst living at Riverside House and my friends and I used to get through a gap in the hedge and nick his chestnuts. Sometimes we were caught and ran away.

My late mother's sister Nora married Albert Goodrum and lived in Buckenham where Albert was a tractor driver for East Anglian Real Property. Their son Derek took over from Harry Hunt as the postman at Reedham in the 1950s, and he lived in a rented property owned by Mrs Effie White, on Middle Hill. He later moved to a council house at Newtown. Aunt Nora and Uncle Albert later moved to one of the terraced cottages on Riverside, between Crouchen's Stores and the Warren.

In 1952 my father applied for the manager's job at Stalham Co-op, was successful, and in December we moved to Stalham. Since living in Stalham I have bumped into several people from Reedham. John Austin, who was the son of the Reedham policeman, became a policeman and was stationed at Stalham for many years. In the late 1960s I used to play darts for a pub in Hickling. When we were drawn against Bird's Eye Social Club from Gt.Yarmouth in the Mercury Cup, the captain of the Bird's Eye team was my old mate Ian Mace. A few years ago whilst working at Herbert Wood's Boatyard at Potter Heigham a young lad came to be an apprentice boatbuilder. His name was Alex Tibbenham. I asked him if he came from Reedham and he replied yes. His grandfather was Russell Tibbenham, who was a son of George Tibbenham, who was once a builder at Reedham.

Figure 18. Two views of part of what was once Station Farm buildings on Ferry Road, supplied by Julie Layton. Top: in the 1960s when the right side was a shed and the out-building at the far right was a toilet and coal house. Bottom in 1970s after alterations and the shed had been converted to a bathroom with running water and part of the land had been sold and a bungalow built alongside on Ferry Road.

Figure 19. Top: The Eagle Tavern photographed in 1964, supplied by Keith Nursey. This is now a private dwelling known as Eagle House. The building at the right behind the pub is where the Nicholls family lived.

Bottom: Florrie and Nellie Browne at the bar inside the Eagle Tavern. Supplied by Myra & Sony Horton.

BRYAN NICHOLLS REMEMBERS:

I was born 20th November 1938 (Dad said Hitler bombing Poland was responsible), the third son of Kate and Ted Nicholls. Brother John was 3 ½ years older and Charlie, who many will remember as Landlord of the 'Shoulder of Mutton' Strumpshaw, was 23 years older.

My first childhood memory was not a happy one, my brother John was knocked down and killed by a van outside our gate, aged 6 ½ years in March 1942. I remember him being laid out in our front room.

At the age of 4 ½, I started school in Mrs Howard's class. My early school days must have been fairly happy as I can't remember not wanting to go. Moving up into Mr Howlett's class brings memories of when his double ruler would come across your knuckles if you weren't holding your pen correctly. From about 9 onwards we were taught by Mr Kingdom and then Mr Cook, both of whom made learning really enjoyable. I recall that at the end of term we would scrape our desktops clean with an Every ready single bladed razor – I used my dad's old cut throat – job done in half the time!

Figure 20. From the left: Mrs Munro, a seamstress who lived on Riverside, Mrs Griffin, and Mrs Kate Nicholls who lived on Ferry Road. Supplied by Bryan Nicholls.

There was no central heating in the classrooms: teacher stood in front of the fire, surprised we didn't get frostbite, but I remember, in the days before school lunches, that we would toast our sandwiches over the fire – they tasted great.
I finished my school days under the guidance of Mr Boast. My last year was as joint school captain with Tony Howard.

There were many interests to occupy ones self with out of school hours: cubs with Akala Yvonne Rednall, scouts, which was taken by John Boast, football matches against other school teams like Freethorpe, Lingwood etc.

I recall the days of when winter was winter with snow that seemed to last for weeks on end. These were the times when we were allowed to have slides in the playground, and a fond memory was at night, when the moon seemed as bright as day, with our home made sledges we would sledge from the top of the railway bridge right down Ferry Road past the houses and round the bend. I remember learning to swim at school, when in early May we would be transported by coach to the outdoor swimming pool at Gt. Yarmouth and the water temperature was only 42 degrees F. - never was a cup of hot Oxo more welcome. Other excursions from the school each week were to Freethorpe School, one week carpentry, the next for cooking lessons.

Figure 21. From the left: Alan Barr, Bryan Nicholls, and Rodney Pettitt at the New Years Eve Party 1952. Supplied by Bryan Nicholls.

The British Legion Hall was used for lots of activities: Thursday nights were picture nights and invariably the film would break down several times each week. Dancing lessons by Mr and Mrs. Birtles from Acle were also popular, although more so with the girls than the boys – still I didn't mind – less competition. Whist Drives and Beetle Drives were also well attended. George's fish and chip shop, next to Legion Hall was a popular meeting place for us youngsters. I belonged to the Church choir for several years, I was not much good at singing but it was another place to meet up with girls. When I was about 10 a favourite place was Reedham Ferry where I used to fish, also helping Arthur Benns to hand crank the chain ferry across the river. If the driver did not have the right money, Arthur would accept cigarettes in place of.

My father, Edward (Ted) Nicholls was born in Limpenhoe in 1888 and moved to Ferry Road, Reedham when he married my Mum at Reedham Church in 1915. He left school at 13 and worked as a farm labourer. I believe he also worked at Cantley Factory during its construction. At the time of his marriage he worked on the railway, and I can only ever remember him working on the railway between Reedham and Cantley as a lengthman. Many a time I can recall as a boy taking Dad his tea when he was on fog duty, real pea-soupers they used to be, and being allowed to fit the fog signals to the rails. They would go off with a very loud bang when the train passed over them. It was in the railway hut that I cadged my fist fag, encouraged by Dad's fellow workers. I don't know to this day whether Mum ever found out. Like most people in the village we were fairly poor and Dad would grow all his own vegetables – he had 2 allotments, one behind the Eagle and one on Parish land off Church Rd. He took great pride in showing his vegetables at the yearly village fete and was very proud when he was successful. He took an interest in the local cricket and football teams and was always a willing helper. After he retired from the railway he worked for Jack Edwards at Station Farm. He died suddenly on May3rd 1957, Cup Final Day.

I believe my mother Kate Dorothy Nicholls, nee Cordy, was born (1897) in Freethorpe, where her father was a policeman, and later moved to Ferry Road in Reedham in her teens and where she lived for over 50 years. Like Dad, she worked hard most of her life to make ends meet, she took in lodgers, did laundry and did cleaning work. Most of the cooking was done on a coal-fire cooking range and all the water required for drinking and washing etc. had to be carried from next door from a pump, which had to be primed, especially in winter with hot water, by the bucket full. Every Saturday Mum would go to Norwich to collect shoes from Yallops Shoes in St Ausustines for customers in the village. I would have to meet her off the train to help carry the parcels and collect my reward – the Mickey Mouse comic.

Mum attended church every Sunday, sometimes twice (morning and evening) and we even had our own boxed pew with our name on it which we shared with Mr and Mrs Curtis of Church Road. Mum was an active member of the Mother's Union, which she joined in February 1930 and enjoyed attending the meetings well into her eighties. For 20 years, during the 50s and 60s she was secretary / treasurer of the Older Residents Club with meetings being held every week in the Church hall. She arranged, via taxis and voluntary cars, to get members to the meetings, where they used to play cards, dominoes, listen to talks or were entertained by people from far and wide. This would then be followed by tea, sandwiches and cakes, all duly supplied by volunteer ladies. To raise funds for this I would help Mother to organise whist drives and beetle drives. Prizes for this were begged from local businesses and friends. Mum was also a member of the British Legion and Women's Institute. How mum found time to do all these things and still look after her family remains a mystery to me. When the house and garden eventually became too much for her to handle, she moved to Brundall, and in her latter days she moved to Springdale Nursing Home. She passed away in June 1989 and her ashes were laid to rest with Dad.

Figure 22. Alfred Leonard Humphrey photographed in 1920 when he had a cycle business located near the Eagle Tavern. Top: inside the workshop, bottom: outside the workshop. He became the landlord at the Railway Tavern in July 1923 and later in the 1930s moved his cycle business across the road into the old 'smithy' after the blacksmith George Sayer finished. He also made the old smithy into a garage/ filling station and ran a taxi service from there. Supplied by Joan Adams, nee Humphrey.

Figure 23. Reedham Bowling Club members. Back row from left: Billy Bottomley, George Sayer, J. Little, G Corke, E. Merry, Cable, Sewell, B. Durrant, Scrivens. Seated: H Boast, Tills, L. Humphrey, D Woodcock, Merry, H. Forder, Harmer. Front: R Howard and C. Mace. Supplied by Joan Adams, nee Humphrey.

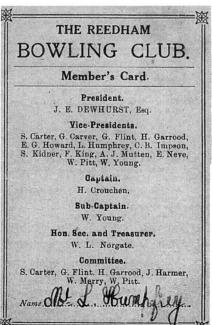

REEDHAM BOWLS.

Reedham Bowling Club having previously had the use of a private green, the tenancy of which has ended, has decided to take steps to obtain a site for a new green. Meetings have been held, and a deputation waited upon Messrs. Lacon & Co., the owners of the Railway Hotel. This firm consented to a green being laid at the hotel, and made a generous offer in the way of financial assistance. The green is now being laid. At a meeting of bowl players, Mr. J. E. Dewhirst was elected president for the coming season, with Messrs. Stanley Kidner, J. Beevor, B. Crouchen, G. Calver, S. Carter, G. Flint, E. G. Howard, L. Humphrey, F. King, and E. Neve vice-presidents. Mr. B. Crouchen has been elected captain, and Mr. W. L. Norgate hon. secretary. The club is enrolling new members.

Figure 24. L Humphrey's 1925 membership card and a 1920's newspaper cutting showing that a bowling green would be provided at the Railway Hotel.

25

Figure 25. Top left: Humphrey business card. Bottom left: Mr Humphrey in his first car in 1924. Top Right: Inside the Railway Tavern. Bottom: On the Railway Tavern Steps Mrs Humphrey, Mr Mace, Wally Mace, Tim Hipperson, 'Bruiser' Mace, 'Showy' Cooper and George Wilson. Supplied by Joan Adams, nee Humphrey. The Railway Tavern closed in 2006.

KEITH PATTERSON REMEMBERS.

I first started work at the Reedham ferry in the autumn of 1958. The ferry was owned then as it is today by the Archer family. The ferry itself was the old boat. The new one came into service in 1985. On the old ferry there was only one drive chain, on the side where the single engine was, and a guide chain on the other side. This meant that when the tide was coming in, to get the ferry in square the ferryman had to pull this side in on a rope, and if the conditions were bad, high winds etc., he had to use pulley blocks to get the boat into position to drop the ramp. On the new boat the ramps are raised and lowered with a hydraulic system, while on the old one you had to raise and lower the ramp manually. It was much harder in those days.

At that time Norwich was still a port and you could expect up to 4 or 5 shipping movements a day, cargos including timber, scrap iron, fertiliser, corn, and sugar from the Cantley sugar-beet factory. Also at that time motorized wherrys would I take sugar-beet to the factory. Each time a coaster came by the ferry had to stop and the operator had to lower the chains onto the riverbed. Although the old ferry was a bit smaller then the present one the lorries carting sugar-beet were much smaller than today's juggernauts and although we couldn't take a loaded lorry the empty return lorries were no problem, and I can well remember the haulage companies that used the ferry. From the Norton side of the river Askew, Gaze, Kidner, Hall, Collins and Keeler, were the main ones and I got to be good friends with the drivers. In those days there were not as many cars on the roads as today. For pedestrians and cycles, rather then take the big ferry over, we took a large wooden boat, which we sculled over the river with a single large oar over the stern of the boat. This took a bit of getting used to and I remember Mr Archer training me to use the oar in a figure of eight movement but to start with he kept the boat tied to the quay head until I had mastered the technique.

Figure 26. Mrs Benns at the front door of the Ferry Public House. The signs above the door read: 'The Ferry. Youngs & Crawshay. Champion Norwich Ales & Stout'. And 'Arthur J Benns licensed to retail beer to be consumed on the premises. Dealer in tobacco'. Arthur John Benns was licensee from 1944 to 1949. Supplied by Joan Adams, nee Humphrey.

The Ferry Inn like all Broadland pubs has changed over the years. Holliday makers now want more from the pub in terms of food. Days of the hot pie and 'toasties' are gone. Customers now want restaurant facilities and high-class cuisine, both of which can now be found at the Ferry Inn today.

Figure 27. Reedham Ferry circa 1950. Supplied by David Archer.

Figure 28. Reedham Ferry Inn circa 1950. Supplied by David Archer.

Figure 29. View from the top of Reedham Ferry Mill looking south west, showing the Ferry and the Ferry Inn. The building on the opposite side of the river bank was once the Cockatrice Public House and the mill in the distance was the Norton drainage mill. Supplied by Malcolm Cushion.

Figure 30. Top: Lister LD1M (Light Deisel one cylinder Marine) diesel engine on the Reedham Ferry. Bottom: Lister Diesel Service Van on the Ferry in 1956. Supplied by Mick Ford who was the Norfolk Service Engineer for Lister Diesels.

Figure 31. Two postcard (J. Salmon) views of the Reedham Ferry. Top: supplied by Malcolm Cushion. Bottom : 1979 supplied by Peter Allard.

Figure 32. Reedham Nurseries Staff Party circa 1950. Reedham Nurseries was located on Station Road and closed in the 1980s. From left at the table: Mrs Turner, Bill Turner, Effie White, Violet Sparkes, Lily Sparkes, Roger Hipperson & Mrs Forder. Supplied by John Hipperson.

Figure 33. Myra Carter inside one of the glasshouses at Reedham Nurseries. Supplied by Myra Rednall, nee Carter.

Figure 34. A view of Riverside in the early 1900s before 'The Nook' was built. Photograph by P.W.Browne and supplied by Myra and Sony Horton.

Figure 35. The wherry 'Albion' at Reedham circa 1950. The building on the right was at the time owned by the East Norfolk Catchment Board and had previously been a mushroom factory, a wine depot for Backs Ltd and before that a maltings. Supplied by Sony and Myra Horton.

Figure 36. Two riverside views. Top: Browne Series postcard (J1074) from about 1903. The building on the right was at that time a maltings.

Bottom: A photograph taken by P.W. Browne circa 1930 after the bungalow called 'The Nook' was built. Supplied by Mike Browne.

Figure 37. Top: A postcard view of a wherry sailing down river with the old Halls boatyard on the left and the Lord Nelson public house on the far right. The Methodist Chapel on The Hills is visible at the top left, circa 1910. Supplied by Myra and Sony Horton.

Bottom: Postcard Riverside view with the Lord Nelson at the centre circa 1954. Supplied by Steve Sanderson.

Figure 38 Riverside postcard views. Top: circa 1940, supplied by Steve Sanderson.

Bottom: circa 1980s, supplied by Malcolm Cushion.

Figure 39. Large coasters heading downriver through Reedham in 1952. Top: Dutch vessel 'Arbo'.

Bottom: 'Acrity', built by George Brown & Co, Greenock in 1934 for Everards of Greenhithe. Broken up in 1964 in Holland. Supplied by Bridget Jex, nee Saunders.

Figure 40. Coasters heading upriver through Reedham in 1953.
Top: 'Festivity', built in 1944 for Ministry of War Transport as Empire Fanfare. Acquired by Everard of Greenhithe in 1946 and broken up in Holland in 1961. Bottom: 'Sonority', built by Fellows & Co of Great Yarmouth in 1952 for Everard, and broken up in Greece in 1986. Photographs by the late John Debbage and supplied by Julie Layton.

Figure 41.Top: Inshore minesweeper HMS Reedham M2723 by The Lord Nelson in April 1959. Supplied by Jim Rednall.

Bottom: East Coast Truckers being escorted along Reedham Riverside. Supplied by Peter Allard.

Figure 42. Lord Nelson public house. Top: circa 1960 with cafe on the right, supplied by Malcolm Cushion.

Bottom: Mr Rushmere, unknown, Clem Spalding and Ben Chase outside the pub. Supplied by Mabel Moore, nee Chase.

Figure 43. The Ship. Top: circa 1890, standing in the left doorway is Charles Mutton and in the other doorway is Maude Mutton and Emily Mutton. Supplied by Joan Adams, nee Humphrey.

Bottom: circa 1930s, from a postcard supplied by Myra and Sony Horton.

Figure 44. Two postcard views of The Reedham Ship public house with visiting pleasure steamers. Top: postcard JS&N6404.

Bottom: Browne series J3917 postcard with SS Cobholm. Supplied by Peter Allard.

Figure 45. Sydney Charles Mutton Coal Merchant. His store was located on Riverside between the Swing Bridge and Bridge House. Top: The early years with his horse and cart.

Bottom: the later years with a coal truck. Syd with his wife Ida. Supplied by Joan Adams, nee Humphrey.

Figure 46. 'Golden Galleon' opposite Pearson's yard in 2006 before being broken up. Bottom: Reedham built (1904) wherry 'Hathor' in 2005.

Figure 47. Top: Riverside with Riverside House in the centre background and the timber yard to the right. The steamboat on the far left is 'Kestral'.

Bottom: Pleasure steamboat 'Waterfly' heading down river from Reedham with the riverside timber yard in the background. Supplied by Peter Allard.

GWEN BODMER, NEE MOORE, REMEMBERS:

My mother and father (Lally Moore) came to Reedham in the late 1920s just before I was born. They had left Lowestoft due to the depression and lack of work. My father managed to get work at Cantley Sugar Beet Factory.

Mum was not too happy about life in a village where sometimes it takes years to become accepted and she was quite a reserved person. On the other hand my Dad was outgoing and friendly and soon chummed up with Fred Buxton, who also lived with his wife and two children (John and Nancy) in Reedham and worked at the Factory. Mr. and Mrs. Buxton and my Dad and Mum became friends for life as did I with Nancy. I still write to her and visit her when I come to England.

I have wonderful memories of Sundays in summer, when we all met at the Ferry with Roger Stone and his sisters Ena and Avis. We would take a picnic lunch and everyone had great fun. Others I recall being there were 'Uncle Tom Carruthers', and another friend named Ray. There was a lot of good -natured banter between the adults and invariably someone was thrown into the river.

At some stage Mr. and Mrs. Buxton moved back to Norwich and my mother then felt more unsettled and wanted to go back to Lowestoft. This we did some time before the outbreak of WWII. My father continued to work at the Cantley Factory and eventually became Chief Engineer, until he retired. War came and my young brother Mick and I were evacuated to Glossop in Derbyshire. After only six months, Mum and Dad decided we should all be together and they managed to rent a house in Reedham. It belonged to Mrs. Corbyn and was called 'Blenheim House' but more affectionately known as 'Mustard Pot Hall'. So Mick and I returned to Reedham School and walked the distance from Blenheim House four times a day .I think the children from Berney Arms must have come by rail to get to school in the winter as I remember once being caught out smoking with them in the station waiting room.

There were only four classes in the school, from aged 4 to 14. Miss Mount, who later married Roger from the Ferry and became Mrs. Stone, took Class 3 and she was an excellent teacher. Mr. Howard, the headmaster took the top class, class 4.

While living in 'Mustard Pot Hall' I was very friendly with Joy and Heather Edwards, whose father Jack, ran the farm close to the station. With Enid Mace and my brother we formed a small group, put on very amateur concerts and fetes and raised quite a bit of cash which was donated to Mrs. Churchill's 'Aid to Russia' fund, and buying bullets for guns, etc.

Mrs. Corbyn decided to return to Reedham and we had to quickly find somewhere else to live, finally managing to get rooms with a Mrs. Palmer, opposite the station and over the Blacksmith's shop. After a few months we managed to rent a cottage in Drury Lane. It was here that I became good friends with Mabel Chase.

I left school and went daily to Norwich, to Underwood's Secretarial College and then work. My social life was in Reedham and I enjoyed the dances held in the Church Hall and the British Legion Hall at the corner of Station Road .

The local boys were good company and we often paired up, it was lovely being escorted home by a boy friend. Unfortunately by the time we were walking home, the 'honey cart' was doing its rounds, which we tactfully tried to ignore. What was worse and most embarrassing was when the cart was actually outside my home - very off putting for the goodnight kiss.

One of the major events of war time was when the American planes crashed in the nearby marshes. My young brother thought the advent of the Yanks in the village was really something but I was still rather young and well protected by my parents with dire warnings about being wary of the forward Americans.

As the war was nearing the end, it was considered safe enough to move back to Lowestoft. This was a big upheaval for me, as it meant I was leaving my friends behind and I had lost touch with the ones in Lowestoft. I married quite young and we lived in Lowestoft until 1980, raising seven children. In 1980 we retired and emigrated to Perth, Western Australia, this resulted in our family being divided, with three staying in England and four in Australia.

Figure 48. Gwen Moore in 1933 outside the semi-detached cottage on Mill Road where she was born. The lean-to on the left was the wash house. Supplied by Gwen Bodmer, nee Moore. The two cottages were later made into one dwelling.

DEREK FORDER REMEMBERS:

I was born in Reedham in 1938 and attended the Reedham School. I qualified to go to Wymondham College and I was the first male pupil from Reedham to attend the newly opened college, and Carol Baker was the first female pupil so to do.

Following my education at Wymondham I completed an apprenticeship as an Engineering Draughtsman at Brooke Marine in Lowestoft: and studied at both Lowestoft and Norwich Technical Colleges and after which I left the area to further my industrial experience and education in the North East where I have lived for the past 48 years. Whilst living in Reedham I was active in the cubs and scouts, played soccer and cricket locally and enjoyed various other interests and activities.

During my time the cub mistress was Yvonne Rednall and the leader of the

scouts was Trevor Chatters, one of the sons of the landlord at the Ship Hotel. Whilst in the cubs I can recall that we made a tableau for a carnival comprising a large paper mache boot mounted on the back of a lorry with us cubs peering through various holes in the boot to represent the nursery rhyme 'The old Woman who Lived in a shoe'. In the scouts I can recall, in particular, a camping

Figure49. The Lilacs in 2006. Hutchinson.

weekend at Paston in North Norfolk when we were all transported on the back of Mt. Pettitt's lorry. For this particular camp Mr. Pettitt also donated a box of skinned rabbits which went into the cooking pot complete with their heads attached.

My great grandfather was George (Tiger) Forder, the landlord of the Ferry Inn from 1884 to 1916. A tale that my parents told was how my great grandfather collected his barrels of beer from Reedham Station by horse and cart and was assisted in the loading and unloading of the barrels by the station porters. My grandfather on such occasions would partake in a few social beers either at The Station Hotel or The Eagle prior to returning to The Ferry somewhat inebriated. On one such occasion the porters decided that whilst he was in the local they would take the full barrels off the cart and replace them with the empties that they had just offloaded. Apparently, when he got back to The Ferry and discovered the practical joke that they had played on him you could hear his utterances from as far away as the station itself.

Reedham Memories

With respect to the school activities my prime recollections are of being the 'milk monitor' when you were responsible for ensuring that each pupil in your class received a bottle of milk each day (in the winter the milk had to be thawed out in front of the open fire), the visiting school dentist aptly nicknamed 'the butcher' and the visiting school nurse with her hair massages in the search for pupils having 'hair lice' or 'nits' as they were called locally. The major improvements during my time at the school were the building of the school kitchen and dining hall when the cook was Mrs. Winnie Ewles (the wife of Billy Ewles who farmed on Mill Road) and the introduction of the school playing field in New Road -this field was conveniently located at the bottom of our garden. On the land immediately opposite the school and on the other side of Low Road we had a school garden which was divided into plots and each plot was allocated to two or three of the senior pupils who would be responsible for its upkeep. The produce was initially sold to raise cash for the school funds and latterly it was put to use in the school kitchen.

I can vividly recall the incidence of an exceptionally cold winter in 1947 when we had rather a heavy fall of snow. The river was completely frozen over and the snow was cleared using a farm tractor from Bertie Dawson's farm, this was driven by Tom Mutton pulling a heavy wooden snow plough in the shape of an 'A'. Several of us youngsters were co-opted by Tom Mutton to sit on the sides of the snow plough to give it added weight and what fun it was for us kids to be driven straight through seemingly huge snowdrifts. There was no salt to put on the roads and even after the snow plough had been applied the roads were still covered by about four to six inches of compressed snow and those fortunate enough to own a car would fit chains to the car wheels in order to get traction and achieve some semblance of control .

At this time I lived in Mill Road where we had no running water or sewage facility, our water was all drawn in a galvanised bucket from a well which was shared by our family and our next door neighbours Mr. & Mrs. Thaxter. In those days Monday was always the family 'washing day' and we would haul buckets of water from the well to fill a large copper under which we would light a fire and keep it burning using any manner of combustible materials that could be obtained until such time as the entire laundry for that week had been well and truly boiled. The laundry would then be lifted from the boiling water using a wooden stick and rinsed in a tin bath full of cold water. The hardest part was then having to turn the handle of the mangle whilst somebody else fed the laundry through in order to squeeze out as much of the water as possible. Out toilet was a rather primitive unlit brick building located at the bottom of the garden and was emptied by the 'honey cart man'. I can tell you that the 'load' from the cart was not always deposited where people thought it was and that it enhanced the colour and flavour of many cabbages, turnips and potatoes grown locally..

In my younger days we always had a 'roadman' allocated to the village and whose job it was to ensure that the roads were free from potholes and that they were kept clean and tidy, well drained and the road edges and associated banks were kept trim. Initially I can remember Mr. Fred Scrivens doing this job and on his retirement he was succeeded by Charlie Dyball, then George Canham and finally Arthur Webb.

As with most places the village had its characters such as:-

Dan Prettyman - selling his watercress for a few pence per bunch - what a pity it has then taken over 60 years for someone to declare that watercress is very good for your health. Also worthy of note is the fact that we collected rose hips in the autumn, took them to the school where a processing company would collect them from us and pay us according to the weight collected - rosehip syrup has also recently been declared good for our health.

Freddie Sparkes -with his dry humour and who always had time to have a little chat with the youngsters.

Similarly a man called 'Chips' Tungate. Hilton Hanton - the honey cart man.

Jack Hunt - the River Yare commissioner who was always to be seen busying himself with the broads holidaymakers attempts to land and tie up a cruiser or yacht in the tidal water.

Nurse Jackson -who always seemed to be dashing somewhere on a medical mission and who must have been responsible for the delivery of every baby in Reedham for a considerable number of years.

Reedham Stores -when the shop was in the hands of Mrs. Cook, and possibly prior to her time at the shop, there was a large glass fronted annex to the shop located to the rear of the present fish and chip shop and the adjoining house and this was used as a drapery and tailors shop. This was discontinued and the annex was converted into a residence until the family moved into the newly built houses in New Road and latterly at the time of Mr. Friths ownership he used part of this annex as a fish and chip shop.

My father was a committee member of the then Reedham Food Production Association and their annual show incorporated a 'childrens section' with various arts and craft categories. This was to me an opportunity for earning a few shillings pocket money and I would enter as many of the categories as possible. I have in my possession today a knitted tortoise with which I won first prize (to the dismay of the girls) in the 'knitted article category' at the age of eleven in 1949- needless to say that it is now a little bit moth-eaten. You will recall that we had no television to keep us occupied in those days!

I can recall the daily passing of an army lorry full of prisoners of war apparently being taken to the marshes off Low Road where they would carry out the task of cleaning out the dykes and ditches. They always waved to us children as they passed and at one time I had pair of slippers made entirely from rope and which were made by these people.

Podgers Cottage on Riverside was named after my late uncle Albert 'Podger' Forder, who once lived there.

Figure 50. Top: The old Mill House and the Corn Windmill. The mill was demolished in the 1910s.

Bottom: Aerial view of the Mill House after the mill had been demolished. Supplied by Malcolm Cushion.

Figure 51. Reedham School photographs. Top: pre-1900.

Bottom: Early 1900s. Supplied by Malcolm Cushion.

Figure 52. Top: Postcard view of Reedham School supplied by Mabel Moore.

Bottom: Reedham School Class 1 in 1919. Supplied by Malcolm Cushion.

**Figure 53. Top: 1935 Reedham School photograph. Back row from left :
Alan Clutten, Eddie Sparkes, Winnie Skoulding, Poppy Marshall, Esmie
Race, Olive Sales, Gwen Moore, Mary Greenacre, Yvonne Harrison, Mike
Browne. Middle: Graham Swan, Noel Powles, unknown, ?Webb, Dick Race,
Gordon Deighton, Harry Sparkes, Leslie McGowan, ?Webb, unknown,
Russell Mace, Unknown, Terry Durrant. Front: Heather Edwards, Tommy
Gibbs, Joy Edwards, Betty Powley, George Powley, Peggy Webb, Barbara
McGowan, Joan Mallett, Jimmy Adams. Supplied by Gwen Bodmer, nee
Moore.**

Bottom: Early 1950's Reedham School photograph.

Figure 54. Top: Reedham School photograph from 1954. Supplied by John Hipperson.

Bottom: Reg Mutton, chairman of the school governors, and John Boast on his retirement in 1975. Supplied by Malcolm Cushion.

Figure 55. Top: Bungalows on Chapelfield in 2006, soon to be demolished.

Bottom: The area where Broadlands Close was built, supplied by Malcolm Cushion.

JOHN AUSTIN REMEMBERS:

I used to live in Reedham and go to the Reedham School. My father was the village policeman at Reedham between the years 1937 to 1949, apart from the time he was recalled in to the army during the war years.

I can remember going to school when Mr Howard was the headmaster and Mrs Howard the infant teacher. Later Mr Boast took over as headmaster. I can remember a boy named Robert Hardisty, who sat in a desk in front of me, getting drowned in the river when he was about 9 or 10 years old.

Figure 56. PC John Austin and Prince Philip at Great Yarmouth in 1986. Supplied by John Austin.

I remember my father telling me that one Christmas Day he and Nurse Jackson cycled along the railway lines to Berney Arms to attend a 'sudden death' in about 1947 or 1948. I remember Nurse Jackson lived with Mrs Thompson near the playing field.

When my father was away during the war my mother and I lived in the police house alone but a young woman named Edie Sparks, who also lived near the playing field, came to live in to keep my mother company.

My father was transferred to a village just outside Kings Lynn in September 1949 when I was 11 years old and PC Flint replaced father at Reedham.

I joined the Norfolk Police and at one time was stationed at Acle, between 1964 and 1966. I recall doing duty at odd times at Reedham, especially when there had been several prisoners escape from Blundeston prison, and I remember one night walking along the railway line from Reedham Swing Bridge to Brundal Railway

Figure 57. P.C. Frank Austin. Supplied by John Austin.

Station checking the empty railway carriages. I also served on the Norfolk Constabulary police launch and several times came to Reedham to drag the river in search of holiday makers who had drowned. These days the police don't drag the river with grabbing hooks but use a diving team.

While stationed at Acle I met and married Judith Manthorpe whose father, John Manthorpe, worked for Frank Sutton, the Acle butcher. John Manthorpe used to deliver meat to Reedham during the war years. After I married I was posted to Stalham, where I remained for 25 years till retiring in 1992. Jack Pearson, who worked at Reedham Coop during the war, was the manager at the Stalham Co-op.

MIKE BROWNE REMEMBERS:

1. POST OFFICE MEMORIES.

I loved the Post Office. When I was young it was such an exciting place to be. There was always something going on from the very first thing in the morning. If you were up early enough you might catch Uncle Neville coming back from 'Dawn Flight' with his dog Duke at heel, his 'twelve bore' under his arm and his bag over his shoulder full of the geese or duck he had bagged that night. Above the kitchen door were notches cut into the wood frame, one for each goose he had shot. The notches almost joined up across the top of the door and were now coming down the sides.

Across the yard the bake-house door was open and the fire in the corner was already burning brightly. The tins were stacked ready. In the big bins the flour and yeast had already been mixed and left to 'prove' overnight. It was now time to cut off lumps of dough to make the 2lb loaves of bread. The lump was dropped into the scale pan, which had been set with a suitable weight. If the pan banged down a piece of dough would be cut off to get a balance. Sometimes small pieces of dough had to be added. The lumps of dough were then kneaded with the heel of the hand into a roll, which was turned and the action repeated. When it had been kneaded enough it was thrown into the tin and sliced along the top with a sharp knife. The tins were lined up on a metal tray and the long handled flat bladed wooden shovel was used to push the tins to the back of the oven. When all the bread was in the oven door was closed and we could take time out with a cup of tea in the kitchen.

Meanwhile in the Post Office a large shelf, which hinged on the front of the counter was raised and propped up by a metal leg. The letters were emptied from the mailbag and my Dad would sort the letters into piles representing the different roads in the village such as The Hills, Chapelfield Road, Church Road etc. The roads were then sorted into the order of houses along the route that the Postman would take.

These 'roads' would be bundled up and tied with string using a special slipknot and put in a bag ready for the Postman's round. The shelf would then be let down to fold flat along the front of the counter and Uncle Eddie would come with damp tea leaves which he sprinkled onto the floor to keep the dust down when he swept. He would sweep the floor dragging the dirt towards his feet. 'That's the Englishman's way' he would tell me and if I ever had to help I would have to do the same. Neville kept pigs. The sties were made of old railway sleepers, which were dug into the ground standing upright to form the walls while the roofs were covered with corrugated iron sheets. New sheds were added from time to time but there was no uniformity in design. The pigsties formed a fascinating pattern of shapes down one side of the back garden. The pigs had to be fed first thing in the morning. Neville had a big 'copper' in which he cooked old potatoes. These were pounded to a mash and mixed with dry offal and water to make pails of swill. Each pail was taken into a sty to be poured into a trough. The pigs could knock you over if you were not careful because they were big and strong and they would push and shove with much squealing to get to a slot in the trough. A big sow once got out when I was there. Neville shouted for me to stop her so I stood my ground in her path with arms waving but to no avail. She went straight through my legs, upending me, and didn't stop till she got to the vegetable patch.

Dad also had another job before he could open the shop. He had collected films for developing and printing from the boats 'down the riverside' the previous evening. These had been sent for processing to Mr. Chadwick at Yarmouth on the last train. Dad collected the processed films and prints, which had been returned on the early morning train. After checking he delivered these to the boats so the holidaymakers could see their pictures before breakfast.

It was now time for the bread to come out of the oven. The loaves had risen to bulge over the top of the tins. Because they had been cut along the top when the dough was put into the tins the crust now hung in two golden ridges at the top of the loaf. The loaves were tapped out of their tins and stacked high to cool before being sold. The scrap bits of dough had been moulded into rolls and baked on a tray. These were surplus to requirements and we could have them. Eddie would get a large lump of butter cut from the 7lb block, which was how the butter came to the shop, and we would spread it thick on the warm crusty bread. What a treat!
And the day had only just started.
The Post Office opened at 9am.

Figure 58. A stack fire at Reedham on the Post Office premises adjoining the Primitive Methodist Chapel. Available water was insufficient but with the arrival of the Acle Fire Brigade and the assistance of villagers it was prevented from spreading to adjacent buildings. The Acle Fire Brigade pump was hand operated, two men a side. They got their water from a well in the Chapel grounds. It was claimed that the fire was started by a spark from a train although the Post Office was some distance from the Railway. This was the claimed cause of many fires. With the insurance money Neville bought a whole load of Fireworks. They were let off, some five at a time, on the Chapel field where the villagers had built a big bonfire to celebrated Guy Fawkes night. Photograph supplied by Mike Browne

Figure 59. Outside Browne's Post Office in the 1920s: From left: Eddie Browne, unknown, Bert Crouchen, unknown. Supplied by Malcolm Cushion.

2. THE REEDHAM PHOTOGRAPHER

My Dad, P.W.Browne, was a Millennium baby born in January 1900. We always knew his age; it was the same as the year. Dad was apprenticed to a Motor Engineers at Lowestoft. He went every day by train. He worked on 'Tin Lizzies', the Model T Ford. He used to say 'Don't get run over by a 'Tin Lizzy'; you'll get cut to pieces by the split pins'. Most of the bolts were secured by split pins.

When he was 18 he was called up and went into Motor Transport. He just missed the War but was part of the Army of occupation in Cologne. German Army Vehicles had been collected together on the Aerodrome and were being serviced before auction as part of War reparations. He acquired a camera and became interested in photography.

After demob he joined my Grandfather in the Post Office business. In 1926 they bought a Model T Ford Tourer. They also needed a delivery Van so they got my Great Grandfather, who was a Coach builder in Loddon, to build a Van body which was interchangeable with the back seats of the Tourer. During the week it was a Van and on Sundays they took off the Van body and replaced the back seats so they could go out for the day.

His interest in photography flourished. He joined the Norwich Photographic Society. The members had a Folio which was circulated. A member would put in photographs and other members would comment on them. He also submitted photographs to their Annual Exhibition and one year he won the Portraiture Cup for the 'Sun Baby'. He proudly displayed the Cup in the shop window.

61

He then started to do photography professionally; mainly wedding photographs. He also started an Overnight Developing & Printing Service; mainly for Broads visitors. He had a dark room at the back of the Post Office. After taking the Wedding pictures he would rush back to develop the plates. These would be washed and dried ready for printing. If he had time he would do some proof prints and take them back to the reception in the hope of getting there before the Bride

Figure 60. Post Office window on The Hills advertising overnight film processing. Supplied by Mike Browne.

and Groom left. On one occasion the plates were blank. He reloaded the camera and rushed back in the hope he could retake some of the photographs but the Bride and Groom had already left. Much to his embarrassment he had to arrange to retake the photographs when they returned from their honeymoon.

When he had a wedding order he would try to do the printing in one batch in the evening after work. I would sometimes help him. The last job was to wash the prints which often didn't happen till after midnight. So they wouldn't stain, Dad insisted that they were washed for half an hour with six changes of water. Because we had no running water we did this in a tin bath under the pump in the Post Office yard. It was a 'cold old job' with sleeves rolled up and arms in the water stirring the prints. Sometimes there was more than one batch to do.

When the prints had dried Dad would spend hours at what he called 'spotting'. With a fine brush (I'm sure it only had about five hairs) and black ink he would put tiny dots on the photograph to cover up any blemishes. He also made colour photographs by tinting black and white prints with colour wash. It was very important to get the colours right so Dad would use a 'shade card' to match up the colours of the dresses. My sister Felicitie remembers going to weddings to help Dad do this. Dad took the photographs of nearly all the nearby village weddings for many years. A photographic friend from London use to say 'Around here it must be inches deep with your photographs'.

My Dad's 'piece de resistance' was a panoramic picture of Reedham village taken from the other side of the river in the '30s. He made a four foot wide black and white print, which he hand tinted and displayed in the Post Office. Recently we had it copied. The man said 'That's amazing; I didn't think they had colour photography in the '30s'. It was so good he didn't realise it was hand tinted.

Dad didn't impress everybody however. I remember when he was getting out his gear to take a family photograph Mum said 'Why don't we go to a proper photographer?'

Figure 61. P.W. Browne. Left using a Reflex Plate Camera to photograph Herons in Reedham Heronry. Right: colouring a wedding photograph. Supplied by Mike Browne.

Figure 62. Top: A painting by Gillian Browne of the inside of the Post Office.

Bottom: Neville Browne's Pigsties behind the Post Office on The Hills. Supplied by Mike Browne.

Figure 63. Local deliveries were often made using barrows and trade bikes. Supplied by Sony Horton.

Figure 64. Gang digging the road on The Hills to lay electric cables circa 1929. On the left is Eddie Browne with a shotgun. These were dangerous times, not everyone wanted electricity! Supplied by Sony Horton.

Figure 65. Two views, in May 1951, of a bungalow on The Hills which was often known as the 'School Master's Bungalow', as Headmaster Mr Howard once lived there. Top: Mrs Florence Witham.

Bottom: Albert and Florence Witham. Supplied by Julie Layton.

Figure 66. Mr and Mrs Fred Cable and Ellen Cable on The Hills with the Methodist Chapel on the left. Supplied by Myra and Sony Horton.

Figure 67. Pettitts Staff Party at Margaret Harker Hall: Seated on the left is Miss Wilson and standing is Mr Schofield. The dancers are Heather Newson, Pearl Woolsey, Yvonne Rednall, Rita Stone, Myrtle Forder, Harry Sparkes, and Stella Ward. Supplied by Yvonne Fransham, nee Rednall.

Figure 68. Top: Victor Pettitt preparing feather craftwork.

Bottom: Some Pettitts employees. Supplied by Malcolm Cushion.

Poultry will solve your meat problem

Pettitts Famous Norfolk Poultry is available to all.
Examples selected at random.

Prime Norfolk Turkeys, 10-11 lb., 70/6 each.
Plump Norfolk Roasting Pullets, 6-7lb., 35/- each.
Fat young Aylesbury Ducklings, 5-5½lb., 30/- each.
Pair of large tender Poussins, 3lb. per pair
(approx.), 15/7 pair. All weights undrawn.
 Delivered free, dressed ready for oven.
As supplied for the Wine and Food Society's Special
Functions. Served at University Feasts for over a
quarter of a century.

Order now for Easter. Ask for details of our Family Food Reserve Schemes.

Pettitts of Reedham Ltd., (Dept. 10) Reedham, Norwich, Norfolk

Figure 69. Top: Advert from the 1950s.
Bottom: Inside the cold store at Pettitts.

CUSTOMERS' ALLOCATION
ORDER FORM

† Use reserves during weeks of scarcity.
† Await my delivery instructions.

STOCK	A Portions per Head (approx.)	B PRICE	C Number required MAX.	D Number required MIN.	E Reserve Required	F Mark "P" for Preference
*PIGEONS	2					
*ROOKS	2					
*WILDFOWL	Varies					
CHICKEN	5					
HENS	6					
DUCKS	5					
GEESE	12					
TURKEYS	15–25					
POUSSIN	2					
TAME RABBITS	8–10					
WILD RABBITS	5					
HARES	10					
PHEASANTS	4–5					
PARTRIDGES	2					
SWANS	20–30					
MOORHENS	2					
GUINEA FOWL	4–5					
COOTS	3					
WILD DUCK	4					
TEAL	2					
WOODCOCK	2					
SNIPE	1					
WILD GEESE	8–10					
PLOVER	2					
CURLEW	4					
KNOTTS	1					
OYSTER CATCHERS	3					
STARLINGS	½					

G Total number of Persons catered for any one week ....

H Total No. of Portions to be Stored. ....

I State if Stock required trussed ready for Cooking ....

* These are usually available every week.　　† Delete that which is not applicable.

Figure 70. Pettitt's Order form from 1949.

Figure 71. Left: Mr & Mrs Richard Berney visiting the Rectory in the 1950s. Supplied by Mabel Moore. Right: Mrs Lawrence, Mrs Kate Nicholls and Rev Lawrence by Reedham Church . Supplied by Bryan Nicholls.

Figure 72. Reedham Church Choir. Back centre: Rev. Lawrence. From left: Unknown, Diane Mace, B. Denny, A Shuttler, Joy Edwards, J. Sparkes, R. Boast, M. James, Linda Taylor, Front: R. Shuttler, John Broom and Mervyn Boast. Supplied by Richard Broom.

Figure 73. Two postcard views of the Reedham Church, 'St John the Baptist', with a thatched roof. The thatched roof was destroyed in a fire in 1981. Supplied by Malcolm Cushion.

Figure 74. Home Guard. Back from left: Neville Browne, Mr Mutton, Mr Race, Mr Howlet, Mr Sales, Mr Cooper, Mr Mace, Mr Tovell. Middle Row: Mr Herbert Walpole, Mr Taylor, Wally Carter, Mr Canham, Freddy Brown, Mr Moore, Mr Ewles. Front: Mr Durrant, Mr Wincup, Mr Ford, Mr Cooper, Mr Collett, Mr Wray, Mr Hipperson, Mr Eddie Browne, Mr Billy Walpole, Mr Plummer. Photograph supplied by Mabel Moore.

RAY WALPOLE REMEMBERS:

1930's SCHOOLDAYS....................I was fortunate to join Miss Mount's class, Standards 3&4, just after she came to the School from Lincoln Teachers' Training College. She was very fit, dynamic and full of personality to appeal to 10 year-olds. We treated her with respect but with an openness that responded to her ideas of making lessons relevant to village life. (I never remember any disciplinary incidents.) She had a happy knack of relating subjects to what we saw and heard around us: no Bill Oddie on TV to prompt us! We learned geography by keeping a log of the cargo-boats going to-and-fro Norwich port and Cantley sugar factory. We noted their names and flags and then looked up in the Yarmouth Mercury their cargoes and destinations. She extended these studies world-wide by arranging for us to correspond with a school in Sheffield and another in Canada. They told us about the prairies, just when the 'Dutchmen' (Van Rossum and others) were removing field hedges. The Hall Road field was enlarged to 100acres, which gave us an inkling of the vastness of the prairies. (640 acres=1square mile: our arithmetic!). In the 1930's the metric system was the Cinderella of arithmetic. Instead, it was the imperial system of pounds, shillings and pence, but Miss Mount managed to bring 'decimals' to life. We knew from our families that the success of the 'campaign' depended upon the tonnage of the beet harvested and their sugar content. It was measured in percentages expressed to 2 decimal places. So we talked of doing 'sugar beet sums'. Older Reedham people approved of us 'Larnin suffin useful!'

Apart from lessons, we had fun learning country-dancing. Miss Mount taught it with such gusto that we boys never felt embarrassed in taking part. She took us up to games on Wednesday afternoons on the new playing field. Sport continued after school, through swimming taught by her fellow tennis player and later husband, Rodney Stone. He lived at the Ferry Inn, where the lesson timetable was governed by tide times. We had to wait until the tide was on the change and there was just enough water for us to stand safely on the narrow ledge of the river-bed along the quay! Only we boys went up with the 'Big Boys' to have practical lessons on the neighbouring School Gardens.

Out of school, we had plenty to do. Many families kept rabbits and chickens to eat or sell at Acle Sale. I don't remember enjoying gathering hog-weed for the rabbits but I did enjoy stick-bundling. Sid Mutten, the coal merchant, sold kindling wood to light our fires. Led by sadly disabled Sid Powley, his brother George, Norman Dodman and I spent happy holidays chopping up railway sleepers and bundling sticks with rubber bands cut from old cycle tubes. Our merriment was fortified by Mrs. Ida Mutten's supply of tea for our breaks in our Station Road shed.

One annual event of our lives was the Sunday School Treat to either Lowestoft or Yarmouth. Here, the highlight was to catch the Southern Belle at Hall Quay and sail to Gorleston. Another adventure, I had with Norman Dodman, was to cycle over the Swing Bridge to the marsh road to Thurlton and thence to Beccles station to see his Dad: without the aid of any maps! The Silver Jubilee and

Coronation were extra-special events for us. We had carnival processions and marvellous village sports filmed by Billy Browne and Fred Burgess , which we enjoyed seeing again and again. I remember transforming my old pram into a coach.

The War brought changes to Reedham with soldiers stationed on the Searchlight Field (now the site of the Village Hall) and London evacuees.

My part-time job was at the fish-and -chip shop. It was started by Paul Nursey's mum and aunt but then taken over by Ernie Spalding. We continued frying in the shop opposite the War Memorial but supplies came from Norwich Fish Market and not from Lowestoft. We were allocated prime halibut which the customers refused. They wanted cod! So next night it was branded 'cod' and we sold out in no time. 'Lovely cod tonight' was a frequent comment, I heard. (My first lesson in retail marketing!) Then in October, fishing from Lowestoft resumed. We were assured supplies from an evacuated merchant whose family was billeted with Ernie. Through this connection, I went to work on Saturdays on the fish market. I was paid wages in fish which I hawked around the village. Suddenly in May 1940 my job ended . On that Saturday morning Lowestoft Harbour was crammed with Belgian fishing boats full of refugees. The full horror of war confronted me as I saw these pathetic families coming ashore with hand-luggage as their only possessions. My life changed dramatically too. Gt. Yarmouth Grammar School, which I attended, was evacuated to East Retford in Nottinghamshire. At the same time we welcomed into our home one of my Dad's colleagues from Cantley Factory, who was evacuated from Lowestoft into our front rooms.

TEENAGER IN WAR-TIME............................Through its evacuation, Great Yarmouth Grammar School resembled a boarding school with its term time self-contained life of its own. However, we did come home for all our holidays. During them I was fortunate to work for Ernie Davidson, who was the area collector of house-holders' surplus eggs. The government urged everyone to keep and sell their surplus eggs to a packing station en route for others' rations So one day a week we collected them to take them over the Ferry to Loddon. On other days we travelled around Norfolk collecting poultry for Pettitts to process. On Thursdays, we went to Acle Sale with rabbits and anything else villagers wished to sell. I was intrigued by the auctioneer taking bids and I quickly learned not to move my head or hands for fear of indicating a bid. As I became accustomed to the auction ring, I was fascinated by Elijah with his long hair curling round the brim of his bowler hat He never seemed to bid while keeping up an incessant commentary, but afterwards he was invariably filling crates with his purchases. Ernie showed me how to watch Elijah scratch the back of his neck, which tipped his bowler to to the auctioneer! Such excursions would seem dull to the modern teenagers, with their continental holidays, but I can still remember the thrill of seeing Filby Broad for the first time and travelling along the North Norfolk coast without a caravan in sight! Social life at Reedham did not seem dull either. By 1943/44 I was working in Norwich with Norman Dodman, Ivan Broome, John Humphrey and Dick Race as train companions. In the evenings we went up to the Men's Club then still called the

Liberal Club. (It was superseded by Reedham Vikings)Here we played billiards, snooker and table-tennis, or chatted with 'Swannie' around the free-standing iron stove. He was an old light-ship sailor who quietly kept the hall running smoothly. Mr. Howard, the headmaster, would come in to play snooker with other adults without any friction from us youths. I will admit that we did not call him by his nick-name (everyone had one). His was 'Cavvie'. How he acquired this derivation of cave-slang for 'beware' I never learned. Of course girls were around but they were never allowed in the Club. Instead they took an active part in the war-time creation of the Youth Club. Pre-war, youth was only on the fringe of Reedham's concerts and socials. In 1944, Norfolk's new Youth Service organised drama classes and a teacher from Yarmouth came to produce one-act plays. This brought us together to form our own concert party. From then onwards, the real heroine was Mrs. Tibbenham, who discreetly managed the Mens' Club's finances too. She was a competent pianist and knew all the hit tunes but, above all, she put up with all our arguments about the productions. Somehow or other Norman Dodman, Anne Symonds, Pat Boyce, Betty Powley, Carol Baxter, Jean Ewles, Eric Farrow, Les Best, Ronnie London, the Rushmers and others fashioned a series of acts into successful productions, and what is more, dear old Mrs. Drewery allowed us to continue to use the Church Hall until the War ended.

JANET CHURCH (nee HIGH) REMEMBERS:

I was born in Reedham, in one of Pettitts' cottages where Dad worked as a cowman on the farm. We soon moved back to Berney Arms, to No 1 Cottage, where Dad worked for 'Yoiton' Hewitt, our authors' Granddad. He lived at Ravenhall, across the river from us, so Dad had to row across for work each day.

Mum (Milly High, nee Hewitt) had been born at No 4 Cottage, Berney Arms, and Dad Fred had been born at Halvergate, so they were going back home where both sets of parents still lived and perhaps they thought it was a good place to shelter from the war. Little did they know that it would in fact be a dangerous place to be when Tucks mill sails caught fire one night and consequently gave the German planes a good target for their bombs. The bomb craters around us were rather too close for comfort, but we were lucky and survived. I remember the neighbours coming to our house that night. The men went to the mill to try to put out the fire, beds were made up on the settee and easy chairs for my brother Tony and myself and the women folk spent an uncomfortable night just hoping and praying no doubt.

Tony and I caught the steam train to Reedham each day for school, as did our parents before us. The thought of little 5 year olds travelling to school in that way fills me with horror. I cannot imagine my children or grandchildren having to do the same nowadays, but to us it was perfectly normal. We also had the Mace family to travel with, but the timing of the train followed by the long walk to school from the station meant we always missed assembly. After school of course we had to walk back to the station and then wait for the 5 o'clock train. I often think of how we missed out on so much of our young lives just wasting time waiting to get home.

Although I loved school and have very fond memories of my time and friends there, I was mortified when I failed the 11 + exam. However Mr Boast, our new headmaster, promised that he would make the school as near to a Grammar school as possible, and I really think he did. He was my inspiration and I am sorry that he has died before I could tell him so. In spite of failing the 11+ I have managed to enjoy a very interesting working life and only retired 2 years ago.

Mr Howard was head master at the school when I started, with Mrs Howard teaching the infants. I still remember my first day at school. After a morning of threading beads and unthreading little squares of material (I wonder what that taught us?) I decided to go home and went to the door through the cloakroom and called for Mum, who was probably back home in Berney Arms by then!

Mr Howard was very keen on his music and he would gather the classes together to sing, with him playing the flute if I remember correctly. I can still remember singing 'Who is Sylvia' and 'Greensleeves'.

We used to take sandwiches to school for lunch, but I remember one day being treated to chips by Mr and Mrs Howard who 'explained' that they had bought too many for themselves.

When Mr Boast arrived he converted a building that I think had been known as the carpenters shop into a lovely new dining room and kitchen where we then enjoyed delicious meals. We all took it in turns to sit with Mr Boast on his 'top table'.

The school Christmas party was the highlight of the year. The partition between the top and middle classrooms would be folded back to make room for the fun and games. I also really enjoyed the trips we took to London etc and later our trip to Jersey.

I remember the shops in Reedham at the time. The Co-op, where sugar and tea etc was weighed out for you, the Post Office, run by the Browne family, that also sold all sorts things, from hankies to shoes at the back of the shop, the greengrocer, where we bought sticks of locust beans for a penny or two and then promptly ate them, unwashed!!

I have lived in Wiltshire since 1967 but I still think of Norfolk as 'home' and the house along the New Cut, where we moved to when I was 8, still crops up in my dreams.

Sheila has done a wonderful job in researching my home area and has given me and my family an interesting record of our 'Roots'. I look forward to adding each one of her books to my collection.

Figure 75. The 1953 floods. Top: Swing Bridge Cottages.

Bottom: The Riverside by Sanderson's boatyard and The Warren.
Photographs by John Debbage and supplied by Julie Layton.

Figure 76. Holly Farm farmhouse in the snow, date not known. Supplied by Malcom Cushion.

Figure 77. The frozen river in 1954 viewed from the Reedham Swing Bridge looking east. Photograph by John Debbage and supplied by Julie Layton.

Figure 78. Reedham Carnival. 1953. Top: 'Dishy' Edwards in the pram and driving the horses of Pettitts Float Billy Johnson and Jimmy Broom. Supplied by Richard Broom.

Bottom: Syd Muttons Float. Supplied by Joe Plummer.

Figure 79. Reedham Carnival: Top 1953 supplied by Joe Plummer.

Bottom 1953. From left: Mr de Caux, Rodney Pettitt, (Gwen Cooper and Mrs Stone at the back), Jill de Caux, John Boast, Hubbard, Mr Macafory at the rear, Forder, Sid Mutton at the rear, Bryan Nicholls, unknown, unknown and Mrs Smith at the right. Supplied by Bryan Nicholls.

Figure 80. Reedham Football Club. Top 1930/31: Back from left: Joe Mace, Freddy Sparkes, 'Bruiser' Mace, unknown, Jimmy Broom, Tom Mutton. Front row: unknown, unknown, unknown, Arthur Taylor, unknown. Supplied by Richard Broom.

Bottom: 1947/48 team. The first time Reedham won the Junior Cup beating Lynn North End. 3 – 0. From Back left: A. Wigget, B. Tibbenam, S. Barker, F. Brown, J. Humphrey, R. Tibbenham, C. Mallett, J. Forder, B. Durrant. Front from left: B. Cooper, D. Hanton, B. Tungate, A. Clarke, T. Baxter. Supplied by Mike Browne

Figure 81. Top: Reedham Football Club 1950s. Back Row from left: Billy Cooper, Freddy Browne, John Humphry, Russel Tibbenham, Basil Tibbenham, Clive Mallett. Front: 'Weedy' Waones, Bro Tungate, S Clarke, B Clarke, Ted Baxter. Supplied by D Rushbrook.

Bottom: Reedham F.C. Junior Cup Final at Carrow Road in 1969: Back Row from left: Tony Etheridge, Jimmy Forder, Richard Croft, Royston Mallett, Malcolm Forder, Brian Elvin, Keith Patterson. Front Row: Paul Spooner, Terry Smith, Robin White, Albert Mallett, Rodney Nixon.

Figure 82. Top: Reedham F.C. Wiltshire Cup Final 1978. Back Row from left: Andy Tibbenham, Gary Blake, David Bane, Jack Bull, Eddie Shreeve, Micky Browse, Robin Tungate. Front Row: Peter Brady, Micky Mills, Rodney Nixon, Albert Mallett, Tony Etheridge, Fred Colk.

Bottom: Reedham F.C. Team photograph from early 1970's. Back from left: Jack Bull, Rodney Nixon, Keith Patterson, Jimmy Forder, John Pegg, Michael Roe, Michael Bedding, Malcolm Forder. Front Row: Christopher Brister, Graham Stokes, Richard Croft, Albert Mallett, Armin Hess, Tony Etheridge.

REEDHAM FOOTBALL CLUB SUCCESSES:

Norfolk Junior Cup Winners in 1948. Runners Up in 1969 and 1976.
Holmes League Cup Winners in 1949, 1950, 1962, 1976 and 1980.
Burgess Cup Winners in 1966.
Wiltshire Cup: Runners Up in 1962, 1974, and 1975. Winners in 1976 and 1978.
Yarmouth League Champions in 1971, 1975, 1976, 1977, 1978, 1979 and 1980.

Figure 83. Reedham Vikings Tug of War team in the 1960s: from the left: Jim Rednall, Clive Cable, John Broom, Geoff Forder, David Woodgate, Neville Harrison, Dick Elvin, Bob Perfect, Keith Nursey and the Neatishead British Legion Tug of War Coach. Supplied by Jim Rednall.

**Figure 84. Reedham Cubs, supplied by Yvonne Fransham, nee Rednall.
Top: The first Church Parade in 1948.**

**Bottom: At the old Church Hall in the 1950s: Back Row: Yvonne Rednall,
Mike James, Tony Howard, Forder, Nev Harrison, Richard Shutler, Jim
Rednall. Front: Bryan Nicholls, unknown, Gerald Harrison, George Steel,
Arnold Rednall, John Harrison, unknown.**

Figure 85. Polkeys Mill and the old Steam Pump house at Reedham Seven Mile undergoing renovation work. Top: 23 September 2005. Bottom: 1 July 2006. Hutchinson.

Figure 86. Polkeys Mill, Seven Mile. Left Millwright Vincent Pargeter attaching sails 30 September 2005. Right: 13 October 2006. Hutchinson.

Figure 87. Ashtree Farm farmhouse, Berney Arms. Top: King Billy Hewitt with his second wife circa 1905.

Bottom: circa 1930. Supplied by John Ling.

DAVID LAKE REMEMBERS REEDHAM &BERNEY ARMS SAILING DAYS.

Figure 88. Cottage 1 to 4 at Berney Arms in the mid 1950s. Supplied by David Lake.

It was in the summer of 1949 that I first became enthralled with sailing, at the time I joined Hellesdon Youth Club, and the Club, with the help of Ken Baker, one of the county Youth Officers, began a sailing section at Hellesdon. Many of us went on a sailing excursion at weekends cycling from Norwich to Horning on a Sunday for a days sailing in Gaff rigged Half Deck boats from 16ft to 22ft. Ken Baker who we all called "Skipper" was a good teacher both on and off the water .

It was at the end of that Summer after attending a two week course at Stalham that the club felt it needed a base to sail from and together with Ken Baker we arranged through the County Council and the Ministry of Works to rent the Mill at Reedham, (from memory I think we paid 2/6d each per month) and thus began for many of us a long association with Reedham and Berney Arms.

Whilst on the Course at Stalham we renovated a 27ft Montague Whaler which through the Norwich Sea Scouts was put in our keeping, we also had a 10ft Sharpie which we built with the help of the County Council, and again it was entrusted to us provided that we took it to demonstrate to other Youth clubs in the County. I remember we took it to Kings Lynn, Denver, and Burnham and for some time ran sailing week-ends on Barton Broad where we camped out on the island which has now sadly gone.

Our first real base was at the Mill at Reedham and during 1950 we dug out a slipway enabling us to keep the boats out of the water, we slept in the Mill and in Tents and life was a continual round of sailing at every opportunity, many times we went from Reedham to Great Yarmouth in the whaler stopping off at

Berney Arms, where we gradually got to know Harry Hewitt the local Farmer, and the Fosters who lived in the Old Inn. The Fosters thought of opening it up again with an Off Licence and a Club Licence, which they obtained in 1952. The Club was called the "Old Inn (Rivercraftsmen's) Club" and I still have my membership card dated 19th December 1952. My membership number was no7. The Club was started and the licence obtained before this as I can remember drinking there before I went in the Army in June 1952.

The granting of the licence was reported in the Yarmouth Mercury at the time and at the licence hearing statements were read out that we needed a club licence and "Harry" went to the court to give evidence and his main theme was that in the heat of summer when he was working out on the marshes he could only quench his thirst by drinking dyke water, the reporter at the court of course translated his Norfolk accent as "Dick" water which was duly reported in the newspaper.

It was in 1952 that I joined the Army and apart from the odd times when I could get leave became an infrequent visitor to Reedhan and Berney. It was whilst I was away that the County Council decided to run their sailing courses from Berney Mill moving operations from Reedham. The courses, then run by the CCPR (The Central Council for Physical Recreation), were well attended but it became a sad time as one of the course members was killed on the river with a collision with the Pleasure Steamer "Resolute". It was on August 3rd 1954 that tragedy struck and a student under instruction, Miss Lily Read, was in a 16ft sailing craft which was struck by the "Resolute" from Great Yarmouth: the craft was over run by the Resolute and Miss Read was killed. At the inquest the coroners jury gave a verdict of accidental death but the Coroner Mr G.L.Talbot expressed the view that if courses continued to be run from Breydon Water he would not be surprised if another fatality occurred. I believe this was the last course to be run there by the C.C.P.R. After this the operations at Berney Arms were rundown and during 1955 all courses there finished. Our own club continued sailing there, and we took the cottage (No-2) on rent and gave up the Mill as a base. We had many lively weekends there, but the accident had changed everything for us, Ken Baker moved away, I believe taking up a teaching post in the West Country, one or two became more interested in other things, and eventually David Pyett and myself took over the rent of No 2. It was at about this time that the Ministry of Works who was responsible for the upkeep of the Berney Mill, in their wisdom decided that it should be opened to the public in the Summer Months, and Harry somehow persuaded us to open it up for him some weekends, eventually a guide was appointed and I think he used to come up from Yarmouth on a Sunday,

It was in 1957 that David and myself bought a 4 ton Blackwater Sloop, she was in a run down condition and we took her to Berney to give her a complete overhaul and refit, we moored her in a creek near the cottage, and over the course of the next year brought her back to life.

We went down most weekends, spending much of the time renovating our boat. We had many people down for weekends, walked for miles over the marshes and the Breydon Wall. It was in August 1955 that I had my 21st birthday party at

Figure 89. Berney Arms Mill in 1974. Supplied by John Ling.

the Inn: that was quite a noisy occasion.

One night when we were enjoying a pint at the Pub we heard much noise from the direction of the River, it was pitch black and there was much revving of engines and shouting, we fixed a light on a motor vessel, the "Doris", coming up from Breydon against a full ebb tide and towing two half Decker's and a motor launch. They were in trouble, and we managed to get aboard her and get the towage secured so that she could berth at the Bemey Arms. The owner, a Mr Adams who lived at St Olaves, was indeed grateful and asked us to sail for him the next day at the Breydon Regatta, it was in the all comers race in his Yarmouth One design with David Pyett at the helm and myself as crew we won the cup for him. I remember we won an all comers cup for him at Burgh Castle, and again at the Barton regatta where I sailed his white boat Jubilee for him.

It was in 1958 that we had to gave up the rental of the cottage apparently they were in a bad state of repair and were to be demolished, it was then that we took the boat on what was to be her only voyage to Holland and back to Ramsgate in Kent.

We set sail from Gt. Yarmouth very early in the morning on the ebb tide. As we left the Harbour entrance the Coastguard station hailed us and asked where we were going, I think we just said "Over the other side". He asked "What is the name of your boat?". This was the one thing we had thought little about and quite spontaneously I shouted out "Vision" and thus the ship had found a name. It was a long trip taking some 36 hours to cross, we had started out in a light wind and as we reached the halfway distance it started to blow. The wind was on our beam and we made some rapid progress, dusk fell and we were in for another night at sea. We eventually saw lights off the Dutch coast, it was about 10 p.m. The Scheldt estuary, and there seemed to be a massive amount of shipping leaving and entering, and we had some quite hair raising moments dodging ships and trying to find the harbour lights of Vlissingen, eventually we saw them heading in and mooring in the outer harbour..

We stayed a couple of days there drying out and sleeping until the weather calmed eventually setting sail for Blankenburg and then to Ostend. A couple more days there and it was time to start heading for home, it had now become very fair weather and then the worst happened the wind fell away completely and the sea became like glass, then a MFV came up to us and offered to take us in tow to Ramsgate which we gratefully accepted. He dropped the tow just off Ramsgate and a very light wind took us in. It was in the outer Harbour at Ramsgate, when I went to fit the outboard, lifting it over the stern and on to the bracket ,that the drive shaft and propeller decided to part company and the bottom half of the engine disappeared into the murky depths of the Harbour. I suppose to this day its where it still lays, unfortunately the engine was borrowed from Norman Archer the Landlord of the Ferry Inn at Reedham, and to put it quite mildly he was not pleased at all when we broke the news to him, however we bought him a new engine and all was again peaceful. Leaving Ramsgate we crossed the Thames estuary and headed home towards Lowestoft. It was in the late afternoon that an almighty storm and heavy weather forced us to shelter near Pye Sands just in the entrance to the Orwell estuary. We rode it out for some hours and with the weather still bad and the forecast not good we decided to go up river to Ipswich where we moored her at the Sailing Club there, intending to leave her and return in a couple of weeks to continue our voyage up the coast to Lowestoft. Unfortunately somebody removed the Mud poles keeping her upright at low tide and she rolled and filled up with water when the tide came in. It was about 10 days before we were informed and by that time she had filled with mud, had lost some of her gear and was in a very sorry state. We really had no option but to sell her and finalise what was to become a closed chapter in both our lives .

I still met up with Harry Hewitt at Acle market which we both went to on most Thursdays, we shared many stories over copious quantities of Tea, and it was on one such occasion that he told me that it would be possible to buy the cottages at a cheap price, I thought about it but decided against it, I was getting married in the not to distant future and felt that it was the more important venture for me, though to this day I have many pleasant memories of my days at Reedham and Berney Arms, it was a lifetime ago but those days are remembered with great affection.

Figure 90. Top left: Henry 'Yoiton' Hewitt, the last man to work the Berney Arms High Mill. Right: Annie and Henry Hewitt at the front door of Ashtree Farm Berney Arms in the 1950s.

Bottom: Frozen river at Berney Arms in 1954 with the pub in the background. Supplied by Julie Layton.

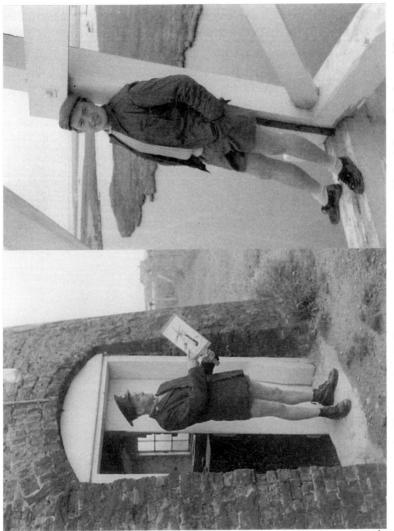

Figure 91. Left: The late David Pyett, a member of the sailing club at the door of Berney Mill in the mid 1950s. Right: David Lake on the fantail extension at the top of Berney Arms Mill. Supplied by David Lake.

Figure 92. Top: David Lake by the old Berney Arms station sign on the railway platform in the mid 1950s.

Bottom: Cottages 6&7 at Berney Arms in the mid 1950s. Supplied by David Lake.

SURNAMES FROM THE 1901 REEDHAM ENTIRE CENSUS RETURNS.

ALLEN	FREESTONE	MARSH	WHITE
ANDERSON	FROSDICK	MARTINS	WHITEHEAD
ANDREWS	GEORGE	MANN	WILBY
APPLEGATE	GAFF	MARSHALL	WINYARD
BANHAM	GOFFIN	MEERING	WITHAM
BARNARD	GOWEN?	MOTAGUE	WINYARD
BARNES	GOWER?	MOORE	WRIGHT
BARTRAM	GRAVENER	MOUGHTON	YOUNGMAN
BARKER	GRAY	MURFITT	YOUNGS
BEALES	GREENACRE	MUTTON	
BECK	GRIMMER	MILLS	
BEDINGFIELD	GRIMSELL	MYHILL	
BENNS	GUNNS	NEWELL	
BETTS	GUNTON	NEWMAN	
BLAND	HALESWORTH	NICHOLLS	
BOAST	HALL	NORMAN	
BOWCOCK	HALLOWS	NURSE?	
BOWLER	HAMMOND	PARISH	
BRINDED	HANTON	PATRICK	
BRISTER	HARMER	PETTITT	
BROOM	HAVIS	PLAYFORD	
BROWNE	HEADLEY	PRESTON	
BRUCE	HEWITT	PRETTYMAN	
BUCKINGHAM	HIGH	PORTER	
BUDERY	HINDLE	POWLEY	
BURGESS	HOLLAND	PURLING	
CABLE	HOLLEY	REEVE	
CHANEY	HOVELL	RICE	
CHIPPERFIELD	HOWE	ROUSE	
CHESTER	HOWARD	RUMP	
CLARKE	HUBBARD	RUSHMER	
CLEMENT	HURRELL	SALES	
COCKERILL	IVES	SARBUTT	
COGGLE	JARY	SEWELL	
COOK	JEFFRY	SHARMAN	
COOPER	JOHNSON	SHEARING	
CORK	JONES	SMITH	
COWLES	KING	STEEL	
CROUCHEN	KNIGHTS	STONE	
CUNNINGHAM	LAKE	TAYLOR	
CURRY	LARKE	TENNANT	
CUSHION	LAMBERT	THAXTER	
DANIELS	LEATHES	TRETT	
DRAKE	LITTLEPROUD	VOUT	
DURRANT	LODGE	WALES	
EDWARDS	LOOME	WARD	
EWLES	LOWE	WARNES	
FARROW	LOWNE	WATERS	
FEEK	LUBBOCK	WATES	
FISHER	MACE	WATLING	
FOLKARD	MALLETT	WEBB	
FORDER	MANTHORPE	WEBSTER	

LIST OF OCCUPATIONS FROM 1901 CENSUS RETURNS.

Agent for Hides & Skins.
Agricultural Labourers
Baker & Postman
Baker's Assistant
Bank Cashier
Banker's Clerk
Barman
Barmaid
Blacksmith
Boatbuilder
Boot & Shoe Maker
Bricklayer
Brickmaker
Butcher
Butcher & Groom
Carpenter
Cattle Drover
Cattleman on Farm
Charwoman
Clergyman
Clerk to Postmaster
Cook
Cowkeeper
Cricket Bat Chopper?
Dairywoman
Deep Sea Fisherman
Domestic Housekeeper
Dressmaker
Errand Boy
Farm Bailiff
Farm Labourer
Farmer
Ferryman
Fish Curer
Gamekeeper
Gardener
General Labourer
General Servant
Grocer / Shopkeeper
Groom / Gardener
Hoop & Hurdle Maker
House Painter
Insurance Agent
Iron Founder & Moulder
Iron & Brass Founder & Moulder
Land Agent

Laundress
Licensed Victualer
Marshman
Marsh Labourer
Miller
Millwright
Monthly Nurse
Mothers Help
Navvy
Newsagent
Painter
Pawnbroker
Plumber & Painter
Police Constable
Primitive Methodist Minister
Private Nurse
Publican
Pupil Teacher
Railway Assistant Bridgeman
Railway Bridgeman
Railway Clerk
Railway Labourer
Railway Permanent Way Inspector
Railway Platelayer
Railway Platelayers Labourer
Railway Porter
Railway Signal Fitter
Railway Signal Fitters Labourer
Railway Signalman
Railway Station Master
Schoolmaster
Shepherd
Stationary Engine Driver
Stockman on Farm
Sub-Office Postman
Tailor
Teacher of Music 'Cert'
Teamster on Farm
Timber & Brick Merchant
Timber Carter
Waterman
Wherryman
Wheelwright
Woodsawyer
Yardman on Farm

Acknowledgements:

It has been a great pleasure to meet up with many people who have lived, worked, and played in and around Reedham and Berney Arms, having been warmly welcomed into many of their homes for a good old yarn about how it once was. I wish to thank them all.

I wish to express many thanks to the following people and organizations for their help in providing valuable information and permission to reproduce photographs, information and tales for this book; without their help this book would not have been possible.

Joan Adams (nee Humphrey), Peter Allard, David Archer, John Austin, Mick Betts, Gwen Bodmer (nee Moore), Richard Broom, Mike Browne, Graham Carlton, Mrs Janet Church (nee High), Alan Clutten, Peter Clutten, Malcolm Cushion, Arthur & Hilda Edwards (nee Riseborough), Mike Ford, Derek Forder, Yvonne Fransham (nee Rednall), Derek and Gillian Havis (nee Browne), John Hipperson, Sony and Myra Horton (nee Browne), Bridget Jex (nee Saunders), David Lake, Julie Layton (nee Debbage), John Ling, Mabel Moore (formally Debbage, nee Chase), Bryan Nicholls, Keith Nursey, Keith Patterson, Michael Pearson, Mike Pickard, Joe Plummer, The late David Pyett, Keith Rackham, Jim and Myra Rednall (nee Carter), Diane Rushbrook, Steve Sanderson, Harry Sparkes, Irene Willimont, Ray Walpole, Ann Wootton.

Eastern Daily Press, Eastern Evening News, Great Yarmouth Mercury, Norwich Record Office, Great Yarmouth and Norwich Libraries.

Special thanks go to Paul Hutchinson for all his encouragement, help with scanning of photographs, and the typing of the book for publication.

Every effort has been made to establish copyright for the photographs used in this book but in some cases this has proved impossible. Anyone with a copyright claim is asked to contact the publisher in writing.

Disclaimer:

Much of the information herein is from people's memories and therefore it may contain some errors as often people's memories are less accurate than they believe, and often people contradict each other. I have tried to check the accuracy but I apologise for any errors that may be present, and I cannot accept responsibility for the consequences of any errors and omissions.

BIBLIOGRAPHY & REFERENCES:

Sheila Hutchinson, Berney Arms: Past & Present, 2000.

Sheila Hutchinson, The Halvergate Fleet: Past & Present, 2001, ISBN 0954168305.

Sheila Hutchinson, The Island (The Haddiscoe Island): Past & Present, 2002, ISBN 0954168313.

Sheila Hutchinson, Berney Arms Remembered, 2003 ISBN0954168321.

Sheila Hutchinson, Reedham Remembered, 2006, ISBN 0954168348.

Arthur C. Smith, Drainage Windmills of the Norfolk Marshes, 1990.

Robert Malster, Wherries and Waterways, 1986.

Robert Malster, The Broads, 1993. ISBN 0850338603.

Roy Clark, Black Sailed Traders, 1961, ISBN 0715354434

Ernest R. Suffling, The Land of The Broads, 7th Edition 1895.

Arthur Stanley Broom, Bob's Boy, 1984, ISBN 09506592.

John Otta Boast, No Idle Boast.

Tom Cable, Crossing the Line, 1991

RG13/1855 Census Records for 1901 held at Norfolk Records Office.

Sheila Hutchinson and Selina Scott in the Berney Arms Inn filming for 'Tales of the Country', 5th October 2006

Other books by Sheila Hutchinson

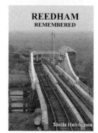